BUDGET TIPS
TO GET YOU THROUGH

Ms Angel Blue

iUniverse, Inc.
Bloomington

BUDGET TIPS TO GET YOU THROUGH

iUniverse books may be ordered through booksellers or by contacting:

iUniverse
1663 Liberty Drive
Bloomington, IN 47403
www.iuniverse.com
1-800-Authors (1-800-288-4677)

ISBN: 978-1-4759-7121-7 (sc)
ISBN: 978-1-4759-7122-4 (ebk)

Library of Congress Control Number: 2013900495

Printed in the United States of America

iUniverse rev. date: 01/16/2013

Introduction

Sometimes, do you feel as if you are working for charity? Do you feel as though you work hard day in and day out and still have nothing to show for your time and effort? Are you letting your money control you rather than you controlling it? Do you need to get your financial situation under control? How can you realign your priorities and learn to take better care of yourself?

Do you find that you are broke all the time? Start valuing yourself because it is extremely hard to value money well. How much money you spend, save, or borrow really does affect your ability to live within your means or beyond them.

Recognizing the issue may help you get back on track to being financially stable. The more money you spend does not equate with your personal value. Money, or having more, neither defines who you are nor does money invest you with power. Real power is controlled by God and comes from within. Having and using your money to feel powerful is a way of seeking external validation rather than accepting your internal worth.

By spending more than half of what you have to spend, it makes a person feel less than what. How could you feel good about your self-worth? People often get carried away. By more out-of-control spending, you may feel self-pity because you don't have what richer people appear to have. This becomes an excuse to avoid looking deeper to sort out what is really hurting you the most financially. Buying only the things you really need and can afford is the key solution. By spending beyond what you can afford, you are self-inflicting pain. This means you are unable to find enough money to pay for new things or items that you have already bought on credit, thus settling for a lifetime of debt for items that you really don't need.

Set yourself on a budget plan and cease to value the bargain. This doesn't mean you have to live poor or shop in the dollar stores; it means learning how to ask for discounts or savings. Some people feel embarrassed to ask for discounts or feel that using discounts shows a lack of generosity. However, people are just deluding ourselves if they feel this way. Our economy thrives on sales and profit; we deserve to get those breaks as much as the next person. Some people have money; some may not have a lot of money. Even if you have a college education and a good job that doesn't mean you give up streetwise common sense!

Women, be aware that a man is not your financial plan. He can be charming, delightful, and even giving. Learn not to depend on a man to pay your bills for you. You need to keep your financial head screwed on firmly and take care of your own financials needs. Do not expect others to do so for you. Being generous to a point of recklessness with your shopping extravaganzas is no excuse. Sticking to a budget plan is neither mean nor miserable, so lead by example.

How could you feel right about a purchase that you have bought? How do you know if it is right of wrong? This includes buying items for your family and the loved ones in your life. Another handout will not help them learn the financial realities.

Never use emergency savings or long-term investments for trouble situations. You are only headed for more trouble if you do this. Many different ways are available to lessen your consumption and thus increase your remaining spendable income. For most people, using emergency savings seems to be the most immediate and realistic option, but you shouldn't sell yourself short on the power of lessening purchases as a longer-term goal.

Keep a log and write down everything you spend money on: food, rent or house payments, utilities, etc. This will make you aware of your expenses and should eventually lead you to spend a bit less(for a few examples such as: close the heat vents in rooms that are not used (such as a spare bedroom), lowering the heat when the family is gone for the day, ect. Don't spend needlessly on items that are not absolutely necessary or that you can prevent with the right organizational skills and willpower. Set a budget, but don't set one that is unrealistic. Set aside some money for real debt reduction. For those who live on monthly fixed expenses and income, take a closer look at food expenditures. You probably don't know how much you are actually spending. Make inexpensive meals that everyone loves. The trick is to buy less you can started out by planning meals or nonfood items? Take an inventory of what household items you already have. Determine what you are using and what you have not used. Put unwanted things on eBay or Craigslist or have a garage sale.

Do you have an obsession with name brands? Being loyal to a brand that provides a quality item that endures make sense. However, you don't have to buy everything that the brand offers. Only a small percentage of people notice what you are wearing. Are you sure you want to impress them? You are only making the clothing company richer. Learn how to focus on getting value and quality for your money, and remember to take quality over quantity.

Credit cards can give a false sense of financial prudence even when you're sliding deeper into debt. Carefully choose which credit cards to keep. This will save you the unnecessary expenses of having too many credit cards and fees. The cost of the cards (some require an annual fee + interest. Whittle down your credit card to allow for a three hundred to five hundred dollar *emergency* fund card and rely on cash transactions. Don't keep more than twenty to twenty-five dollars in cash to avoid impulse buying large purchases. Use debit cards for everything else. Keep track of your spending to avoid incurring debit card fees.

Beware of the temptation danger zones. These include convenience stores that are open 24/7, sales, and fast food chains. Avoid being tempted to buy things out of catalogs you receive in the mail by tossing them into the recycling bin. Don't go out and buy a laptop computer because you have extra money on hand. Be cautious about buying bargain hunter and sales items—a bargain saves even more money if you don't buy it at all. While at work or traveling, if you left something at home that you seldom use, do without it.

Each month, plan a no-spending day. You might wonder how you can make do with the food and resources you already have at your disposal. But give it a try, and see how fast it can turn into a habit. We are often generous with our money, and many people can't afford to do so. Instead, gift others with your time. Check your spending to see how generous you are. If your finances are a concern, set a realistic limit on giving, such as 10 percent of your income.

We need to learn to behave like someone who is genuinely rich—not like someone just playing the part. Drive a harder bargain. Become a smarter customer. Start small, set goals, and reward yourself with something other than shopping. Start saving your loose change in a jar. When it is full, take it to the bank teller. Don't use the machines that charge to take coins asthat defeats the object of saving. Buy clothes and shoes only when you really need them, and calculate how much longer you will use them and their lasting power. Avoid impulse shopping. Buy cheaper items you need (facial tissue, bathroom tissue, tin foil, paper towels. Also store brands (bread, butter, milk, eggs) are often more expensive than the national brands (Wonder bread, Land O'Lakes butter, Kemp milk ect. Are more expensive that the chain grocery stores' products.

Don't go overboard for holidays; be realistic and stay within a budget. Buy gifts that you can afford, not gifts that you buy to please other people. Remember, it is your money, and you must live after the holidays.

Chapter 1

The rich spend too much! Consumer spending is chronically excessive. Many feel they can buy whatever they like simply because they have the money to spend. Stop making your shopping pleasurable and entertaining. This is a sign that you are spending needlessly and out of control—perhaps excessively.

Spending money should be viewed as a necessity. Money should be spent wisely, not foolishly. You may feel that you are rich and have so much money in the bank that you don't need to save or invest any more money. That still doesn't guarantee that one day you might end up broke. If you can't control the way you spend, you could end up poor. Learn how to control yourself when you see items that tempt you—cars, houses, jewelry, clothing, shoes, etc. It is vital to cut pointless spending that will bury you in debt. You must learn how to fight temptation. As much as possible, avoid going into stores when you feel lonely and can't find anything else to do.

You can start by keeping track of your spending. Total your credit card bills to determine how much you have spent this year and last year. Determine the difference. Keep track of how much you spend each day and for what items. Write down the last date you went shopping, and give yourself a grace period in between purchases. Every time you use your credit card, write down the date to get a feel for how often you use the card. Remember, when you use your credit card, you are only borrowing the money, and it is only a loan. Cut up all your credit cards except one for emergencies and don't get more for at least six months. You will see a notable difference in your banking account. Learn to stay away from people, relatives, or friends that influence and encourage you to spend.

I often hear people talking about the number of bills they have a month. Avoid bills that you don't need. For example, maybe you could lower your TV bill by reducing the number of channels you receive. The rich and the poor have one thing in common when it comes down to money: they often say, "I work too hard for my money to spend it foolishly." But people also say, "I can spend my money any way I want to spend it." You can treat yourself, but don't go to the extreme. Take an inventory of all your spending activity. Start by going over your household expenses, what you need to survive, and then your other house expenses. Learn how to say "no" when it comes down to spending money unnecessarily. No one can make you spend money other than yourself. Maintain control over your money at all times.

Stop making shopping your life. Stop shopping for senseless things you don't need and probably don't really want. Shopping can become a habit if you let it. Find constructive things to do with your time instead.

Take a look at our society. Then ask yourself how the poor manage on such low budgets. Regain your independence and take control of your life.

How can you window shop and not buy the things you want? The purpose of window shopping is *not* to spend money. Shopping malls have a variety of different stores that you can enjoy while window shopping. Don't be in a rush and take your time. You can plan to buy some of these things in the future. The objective is not to buy it at that time. Window shopping is not a chore; relax and enjoy yourself and the view.

Live within your means. Can you pay for what you want without using a credit card to pay for it? Live well below your means and establish substantial savings. In today's society, a growing number of people live far beyond their means in an effort to be something they are not or to keep up with the "Joneses." Some people strive to impress their peers with some of the finer things in life such as new, expensive cars. It's easy to spend more and more money each year—money that we don't have to spend—on jewelry and name-brand items to impress other people.

Are you living on credit cards to support your spending habits? Are you on a fixed income and living from paycheck to paycheck? Are you still buying things that you know are not in your planned budget? Trying to fit into a lifestyle that you cannot afford only puts you deeper and deeper in debt. Eventually, you will have to pay the consequences. Learn how to get on a budget plan and decrease your debt.

Start paying for everything out of pocket with cash. Cut up your extra credit cards!

When you want something, learn how to save for it. Learning to save money will save you lots in the long run. Be wise and not foolish! Don't go broke.

Chapter 2

What are the differences between being rich or poor? Most people wonder why the rich continue to be richer and the poor remain poor. Successful people produce amazing results in their lives; the poor live in poverty. Poor people often say it is luck, but being rich can be the result of hard work and not wanting to struggle for the rest of your life. Start by having the right mind-set.

The right habits will lead you toward the lifestyle of financial abundance that you desire. Rich people create a lifestyles while the poor feel sorry for themselves and ask why they can't get ahead in life. Be in control of your life and recognize the actions you are taking for the future. Handling one money takes knowledge. People often make up excuses for being poor and blame others for their downfalls in life. Your circumstances are only temporary. Don't let it be a long setback. You can do better if you strive to do better. In life, you can lose power quickly and lose control when things are not going the way you planned. Take responsibility for the actions you have taken. The rich invest money in stock and bonds; the poor have no money to play around with. The poor are too afraid to gamble with our life savings.

What opportunities does a poor person have in life? Think of the bad situation you are in, and then think of a way to get out of that situation. God gave all of us knowledge; it is up to us to use it. We are not crazy, poor people. We just need direction along with a little guidance and pushing to get ahead. Everyone has big dreams. Some have big dreams of being rich one day. Being committed to your dream means you will do whatever it takes to make the dream come true. Don't waste time on dreaming how it would be if you were rich or how it would feel to be rich. You must have faith in yourself. Your visions and your dreams are the reality of life. You will not stop till your vision or dream comes true. Never give up on life and the things in life that you can have. Don't get upset when God is blessing the next person, "remember" your time is coming one day to. God blesses all us according to his will and planned for your life. Many rich people were born poor. Most millionaires were self-made. They didn't have luxuries while growing up. I am not referring to people who inherited wealth and money from their ancestors. What are rags to riches? God wants us to prosper, but God's ways differ from those of the world. We must first clear our minds and the way we think. We need to change our long-established thought processes from the world's methods of prosperity to God's laws of prosperity and success. We will face many obstacles that enable us to make the right choices. We must have spiritual insight to see our way out of seemingly unsolvable problems.

To be debt free, start eliminating expences and devise a plan to accomplish that goal. Look over all of your bills and credit card payments and determine which ones will be the easiest to pay off first. After carefully looking over your household budget, make a plan that fits your family or you.

Set the money for your bills—rent or house payment and utilities—aside. Then see what you have left over for credit card payments. Read your monthly statement to see what card has the lowest balance. Make a plan to pay more on that card in order to eliminate it first. Work your way from the cards with the lowest balance to those with the highest balance. Keeping to a budget is a structured way to deal with your money and pay off debt. After paying off one debt, increase the amount you pay in order to pay off the next bill. Set yourself a time limit to pay your debts off. Don't try to do everything at once. Set realistic goals to accomplish it. Do not overload yourself and neglect other obligations to get rid of debt. Continue this process until all your debts are paid in full.

After paying your debts off, don't make new ones. Keeping to a budget can be fun, and you can really enjoy being on one and seeing your progress. Learn how to manage your hard-earned money. I'm not suggesting that you do not spend some of your money. But it is important to learn how to save to get the things you want without putting yourself in major debt again. Once you are out of debt, you will not want to go down the pathway of debt all over again. Money cannot buy happiness or a place in heaven. (Philippians 4:19)

Being grateful is a special opportunity to express our gratitude to God for his provisions and blessings throughout the year. Are there any needs in your life that have not been met?

God will provide for all your needs; you must trust him in words and deeds. God promises us that he will not give us more than we can handle. When we are struggling, we can still trust God in the midst of the storm. We are going to face many days with overwhelming trials and tribulations. God will deliver us from them. We can always think about the goodness of God and get instant joy. There's power in the man of God!

When your bills exceed your paycheck, and you don't see any way through this, you can count on God to pull you through. God is your ally; God is your strength in time of trouble. No matter what situation you are in, you still must trust God. Only God can help us in life. Have faith. God hears us. Confess to God; talk to him one-on-one. Find a quiet place alone and pray. When you wake up in the middle of the night, talk to him. God will hear you calling on him, and he will answer.

God will never leave you nor forsake you; he will be with you till the end of time. God cannot break promises to his people. He's a just and merciful God; he cannot lie. He cares for all his children. He pities us with mercy; he is ready to forgive us at all times. His mercy and grace endure a lifetime. He reigns over the just.

I will not serve a God if he was not there when I needed him. God will pour out so many blessings that you won't have room enough to receive them all. We are nothing but blessed! We are the seed of Abraham, our forefather. Abraham's blessing was passed down to each generation. My children and your children will inherit theis blessing.

Why do people get upset when life is not going the way that they want it to? You cannot put a time limit on God. God blesses us according to his will and plan for our life at that time. Your friend's blessing is not your blessing. You don't know how long your friend has been waiting on his or her blessing from almighty God. He doesn't move when you want him to, God is not insist. As humans, we want everything to be given to us right away.

We must learn how to be patient. God never promised that every day would be sunny. We must take the rainy days along with the sunny ones. God is a just and merciful God; he is very slow to anger and pities us with mercy.

While family and fake friends may turn their backs on you, God is always there for you. When trouble comes your way, and you feel that no one cares about you, turn to God; he is always there for you. I can't promise that you won't cry before God comes to your rescue. Crying sometimes helps heal a broken heart. No problem is too big or small for God, and he is always there for you! I am a living testimony.

I have walked and talked with the Lord many days and nights. I gave all my problems to God, knowing that God is in control of all things. Sometimes we need to be reminded that God will never leave us. By going through hard times, we come to appreciate God's grace and mercy.

Remember, Jesus taught that man cannot serve both God and money (Luke 16:13 or Mark 8:34. What shall it profit a man if he gains the whole world and loses his soul to Satan?

Nothing.

Ms. Angel Blue, was born on July 31, 1965, in a small town in Florida. My father and mother had eleven children; I was the youngest. We grew up with little or nothing. My father worked for the local ice plant, and my mother worked in the groves. With little education, they were forced to take any job they could get at the time. My mother completed the eleventh grade, and my father went no further than the ninth grade.

They married in the small town of Edison, Georgia, when they were very young—my dad was fifteen and my mom was seventeen. After about two years of marriage, their first child, a daughter, my older sister, was born. After that, my father cheated on my mother with many different women in the town. My father's multiple affairs resulted in his fathering forty-three children.

We probably would have had more in life if he didn't have to support us as well as his other children. We suffered and were limited in life due to his infidelity. We grew up poor and had very little. As I grew older, I learned not to take money for granted. I learned to spend wisely. Every penny counts. When I see people using money foolishly, I get upset. So many families all across the world are in need of so much.

A person must go through difficult times in life to have a testimony—and this is mine. God bless you that you would bless someone else in need. We are all one body in Christ. We need to learn how to aid one another in need. That's the spirit of God. I do believe every word that is written in the Holy Bible. In his words, God said, "Heaven and Earth will pass away but never my words." I am blessed to have gotten to know God and his son Jesus Christ, my Lord and Savior.

Father God, in the mighty name of Jesus Christ, my Lord and Savior, I come before you. May this book be a blessing and help someone get out of a troublesome situation. May this message be passed on to generations to come, providing its readers hope and salvation through any crisis. I truly pray that this book will help someone not only accept God and Jesus Christ as his or her Lord and Savior, but to advance to seek who they are. I hope it will open up the ears of those who cannot hear.

God has the voice and the eyes of those who cannot see the light. I pray that this book will bring not only hope and salvation but also be a deliverance of recovery to all the readers of this book from generation to generation. Thank you, dear Lord God, for allowing me to write this book. Blessings to all in the name of the Lord Jesus Christ. Amen!

Printed in the United States
By Bookmasters